B
CAS

330691

Minooka Community High School
District 111
Channahon, IL 60410

P9-DIJ-082

KIERA CASS

ALL ABOUT THE AUTHOR™

KIERA CASS

EDWARD WILLETT

ROSEN
PUBLISHING®

New York

Published in 2015 by The Rosen Publishing Group, Inc.
29 East 21st Street, New York, NY 10010

Library of Congress Cataloging-in-Publication Data

Willett, Edward, 1959–
Kiera Cass/Edward Willett.—First edition.
     pages cm.—(All about the author)
Includes bibliographical references and index.
ISBN 978-1-4777-7914-9 (library bound)
1. Cass, Kiera—Juvenile literature. 2. Authors, American—20th century—Biography—Juvenile literature. 3. Authors, American—21st century—Biography—Juvenile literature.
I. Title.
PS3603.A8678Z95 2015
813'.6—dc23
[B]

                                                                            2014010966

Manufactured in China

CONTENTS

Although still in the early stages of her career, Kiera Cass has enjoyed the kind of success most writers only dream of. After publishing her first novel, *The Siren*, in 2009, she went on to write *The Selection*, a dystopian young adult novel set in a future version of the United States in which girls are selected by lottery to compete for the position of Princess. Whereas she had had no luck at all in finding either an agent or a traditional publisher for *The Siren*, *The Selection* landed her, in short order, an agent and a three-book deal with a top publisher.

The book came out in April 2012 to great acclaim, and soon

Kiera Cass never planned to be a writer, but thousands of fans are glad she found her way to it.

found its way onto best-seller lists around the country and the world. The second book in the trilogy, *The Elite*, did even better, debuting at number one on the *New York Times* best-seller list. The final book, *The One*, published in May 2014, completed the story begun in *The Selection*. But it is still only the start of Cass's writing career. She is already working on her next project, a duology about a future where children are raised to be ideal companions that parents can buy for their own children.

Despite her success, Cass remains down-to-earth, a devoted mother to her two young children (who came into the world concurrently with her books). She likes to point out that she may be a *New York Times* best-selling author, but she still has to change diapers and do laundry.

What makes all of this even more remarkable is that being a writer was not something Cass dreamed of as a child or even as a young woman. She began writing as a form of therapy to help her cope with tragedy.

Now she says she can't imagine doing anything else. For that, her legions of fans are grateful.

A PROUD CHILD OF THE '80S

Kiera Cass was born in South Carolina on May 19, 1981—as she puts it on her website, "a proud child of the '80s." Her father was Puerto Rican, and her mother was from the South, but despite that combination, she says she has neither a Hispanic or Southern accent.

Cass says she was awkward growing up: that she "didn't understand fashion at all" (she claims she still doesn't, although she loves the fantastical ball gowns that grace the covers of her novels) and that she "was never into what was cool while it was actually popular." But she also says she didn't mind it much because she had a few really great friends. And although she wasn't interested in writing, she had many other interests: by high school, she enjoyed

Kiera Cass was born and raised "a proud child of the '80s" in the southern coastal state of South Carolina.

dance, theater, and singing. She even sang in a chamber choir that once tied for third in the nation in a competition.

As she told the blog the *Literature Lion*, "In high school I was a choir geek. I wanted to go to Broadway, and I studied music, dancing, and acting like crazy. It's for the best that it didn't pan out. I wasn't very good!"

Even though young Kiera wasn't interested in writing, there was perhaps a predisposition to it in the family. Her mother wrote poetry, and so did her grandmother. Both of her grandparents were teachers. Despite that, "I definitely wasn't pursuing it. It never really seemed like an option for me," Cass said in a 2013 interview with the *Manila Bulletin*.

Minooka Community High School
District 111
Channahon, IL 60410

KIERA'S FIRST CRUSH

On her blog, Cass tells this little-known fact about her childhood: When she was in fifth grade, she had her first celebrity crush...on Bart Simpson:

Even though I had to be something like 10 or 11, I still couldn't process the fact that he was a cartoon, therefore not real, and that the ability for us to actually be together would require Easter Bunny-like levels of magic.

Cass says it took months for her to figure that out, and all that time, she was wearing her Bart Simpson watch to school. She thought she was normal because all the other girls had celebrity crushes, too.

"And now I live with people in my head whining to me about telling their stories," she concluded. "Turned out fine."

DIVA

When she was in high school and people asked her what she wanted to be, Cass says on her blog, she always answered "a diva." In fact, she says, in her high school senior yearbook, half of the signatures start, "Dear Diva." And when she left high school, she was still focused on performing. After graduation, she took a semester off, performing in several

MUSIC TO WRITE BY

Although she gave up on the idea of being a diva, music still holds a dear place in Cass's heart. She creates playlists to accompany her writing process. Music, she says, can "really make a scene happen." She offers prospective writers some suggestions on using music to accompany the writing of their own stories.

First, she says, don't necessarily listen to music that you like. She thinks it helps writers to hear fresh lyrics and melodies, things they might not pick up on their own.

Second, she says, "Writer's Butt is a real thing." Rather than just sitting at your desk, put on your headphones, turn on your music, and take a walk. Along with the music, the new sights will get your mind going.

Third, she says, instead of trying to make a playlist for an entire story, try making one for a single character. Creating a playlist for a character can help you get into that character's head, and get his or her voice right. You might like Broadway musicals, but it's possible your character likes heavy metal.

Fourth, she suggests making mood mixes to help you capture the emotional flavor of the scene. She says she has mood mixes for love, anger, and sadness. Her suggestions? For love, "Dark Blue" by Jack's Mannequin; for anger, "The Pretender," by Foo Fighters; and for sadness, "The Special Two," by Missy Higgins.

local shows and teaching at a theater camp. As she noted in an interview with the *Daily Quirk*, "Writing wasn't even on my radar…Just goes to show, you don't have to have your life planned out at eighteen."

After that semester off, she enrolled at Coastal Carolina University. Her major? Musical theater.

When Kiera arrived at Coastal Carolina University, though, she discovered that studying musical theater wasn't as much fun as performing in it. In a 2010 interview with *Writer's Digest*, she said,

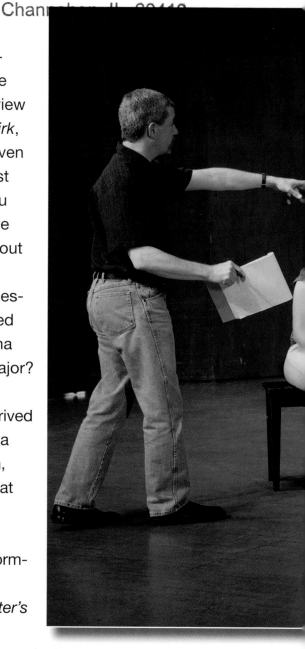

"When I went into musical theater, and I was graded on the way I played piano and had a requisite number

iera Cass's first love was performing, especially in musical theater. Like these spiring actors, she spent many hours rehearsing.

of pieces to sing and all these technical things drilled into me over and over, it kind of sucked the fun out of it. I'm kind of glad I didn't study creative writing when I was younger. I think it would have ruined it for me."

A FANTASTIC MISTAKE

And then, she made what she calls "a fantastic mistake" and followed a boy she had fallen in love with to a different school—and state. From Coastal Carolina University, she moved to Radford University in Radford, Virginia.

Her college years, she told the Filipino blog *I Am Meg*, were turbulent times. Whether or not it was the boy she followed to Radford she didn't say, but in that interview she talked about a boy she was "mad crushing on," even though he definitely wasn't the right guy for her. "But then there was this other girl," she said. "I thought he was into me, but it kind of seems like he was into her. She and I had this really honest conversation about where things were going. I was like, 'I kind of hope he ends up with you,' and she was like 'I kind of hope he ends up with you!'"

Cass noted that she and that girl are still friends. In fact, the other girl married the boy she had the crush on. Cass told the story to make the point that girls can be civil to other girls, unlike the way it is sometimes portrayed in television, movies, and books. "Making another girl seem small doesn't make you seem any bigger," she said. That attitude would play an important part in the character relationships in her best-selling novel *The Selection*.

SWITCHING MAJORS

It wasn't just her crush on the boy she followed to Radford that didn't survive the move to the new college. Neither did her musical theater major. She switched to music. Then she switched to communications. ("But things were never properly communicated to me," she says, "so I got out.") Finally, she settled on history.

"Maybe a year into college, I was over theater (though I still love performing) and decided that what I would really like to do was go on staff with the campus church and just be helpful to students," she writes on her website. She says she settled on history because she could finish it on time after so much switching of majors, and because she liked listening to the stories…little realizing, at the time, that eventually she would be the one telling the stories.

As a history major, she had to do a lot of reading, writing, and researching. Looking back now, she feels the fact that a lot of the real-life stories she had to study have their own twist to them

In what she calls "a fantastic mistake" that shaped the rest of her life, Kiera Cass followed a boy she liked from Coastal Carolina University to Radford University in Radford, Virginia, seen here.

has helped shape her books. All in all, she says, she's glad that she studied what she did because she thinks if she majored in English, she quite likely might have been burned out on reading and writing and might never have pursued a writing career at all. As she told *Writer's Digest*, "I think there's something to be said for majoring in some-thing that will make you money and minoring in something you love."

A NATIONAL TRAGEDY

In the autumn of 2001, Cass's sophomore year at Radford University, the major of the

Minooka Community High School
District 111
Channahon, IL 60410

On September 11, 2001, terrorists crashed two passenger planes into the World Trade Center towers in New York City. Kiera Cass, a resident assistant in her dorm at Radford University at the time, found the news "overwhelming."

moment was communication, and she had become an RA—a resident assistant. "I was excited about the possibility of mattering to someone," she writes on her blog.

She was living on the second floor of Bolling Hall, in a room she says was shaped oddly, kind of like a large closet. The walls were covered with artwork she had painted herself—not very good, she admits, but she liked it anyway. Decorating one wall were several copies of *Playbill* (the theater magazine that doubles as the program for Broadway shows). Back in May she and her best friend from high school, Tara, had taken a road trip to New York, just days before Cass's twentieth birthday.

On the morning of September 11, she went to her first class, an English class where the topic was irony and war poetry. The class ended at 9:15 AM. It took her less than five minutes to walk back to her dorm. As she entered the building, she met one of her residents coming down the stairs. The girl told her to turn on the TV because a plane had just flown into the World Trade Center. Cass did so and saw the footage of the second plane hitting the towers over and over again.

She writes on her blog that she found

Commemorative tiles mark a chainlink fence in New York City in response to the September 11, 2001, terrorist attacks. Like many Americans, Kiera Cass felt a renewed sense of patriotism in the wake of the attack.

the experience overwhelming. She remembers talking to her parents but doesn't remember what was said. She remembers dry-heaving in the shower. She remembers being terrified because, as an RA, she was supposed to be a leader, but she had no clue what to do. After hearing about the attack on the Pentagon and the plane that crashed in Pennsylvania. "I remember worrying there would be more," she writes.

She stayed in her room all day with the door open, except for when she went to get food. She says she doesn't remember crying much, but she thinks she must have because ordinarily she cries easily. In the end, she feels that whole hours somehow vanished from her memory.

Because she was on duty, she had to stay in the building from 6 PM that night until 8 AM the next morning, in case anyone needed anything—but she doesn't remember anyone needing anything. She does remember there was a drum circle in the quad outside her building. "I listened to the drums a long time, and wished I could go out and play myself, if only to do something," she recalls.

One of the things that has stuck with her in the wake of the September 11 attack, she writes, is a sense of patriotism. Even though she says she knows the United States is far from perfect, "It is kind of amazing," she writes. "I'm so grateful for my freedom, and I'm mindful of the people who we lost in someone's desperate attempt to ruin it. I'm still thankful, and I remember."

The September 11 terrorist attack would not be the last national tragedy that Cass found herself deeply affected by. The second would have an even more profound impact because it hit closer to home. It would also be the impetus that finally turned Kiera Cass into a writer.

TWO

FROM TRAGEDY, A NEW BEGINNING

At the time of the September 11 attacks, Kiera had either just met, or was about to meet—she's not sure which—a young man named Callaway Cass. He wasn't on her radar at the time of the attack, but he soon would be. On her website, she describes him as a guy she kept rejecting but whose heart was set on her. She also notes that, of all the things in her life that didn't work out, the one she is most grateful for is following the other boy from North Carolina to Virginia. It was there, she writes, that, "After three kiss-free years, I kissed the man who would become my husband."

Kiera and Callaway were married in early 2004. They didn't have much money, something Kiera commented on in a blog post a few years later. She listed a number of things she loves about her husband that she has added to a book for as long as they've been married. She notes that in their first year of marriage they couldn't afford to get cable television. That was the year the Summer Olympics were in Athens, and Kiera was sad about not being able to watch it. Callaway went out and got a television antenna so that they could at least get two stations, one of which was carrying the Olympics.

Callaway presumably didn't have much money while still a student, either, since one of the other things Kiera notes is that when they began dating, he went out and bought strawberry Pop-Tarts so that there would always be at least one thing for Kiera to eat when she went to his apartment.

After finishing college, the Casses moved to Blacksburg, Virginia, where Kiera was prepared to settle down to be a good homemaker and stay at home with their kids when they had them. She was a college graduate with a degree in history, but she was fine with the idea of being a homemaker. "I was cool being a mommy, I was cool being a substitute teacher for a little while. I was working in an ice cream shop when I started writing. I was okay. I was working to buy books," she told the blog *Ron Reads* in 2013. It might sound dull, but she says the pace of her life was kind of soothing and she has no complaints.

As she told the *Philippine Star*, "It was fun to work at an ice cream shop because nobody comes in angry. Everybody always comes in a good mood. It was really nice. I always smelled like cinnamon and vanilla...I was just working, and keeping the house."

But then in 2007, Kiera was strongly affected by another national tragedy—this one much closer to home.

VIRGINIA TECH

Kiera and Callaway were living near the campus of Virginia Polytechnic Institute and State University, better known as Virginia Tech. Callaway was working on campus at the time, they were attending a campus-based church, and

iera Cass's husband, Callaway Cass, comforts her on Wednesday, April 18,)07, at a memorial on the Virginia Tech campus for victims of a gunman who lled thirty-two people on campus and then committed suicide.

Kiera's friends were mostly students at the university.

On April 16, 2007, the deadliest shooting rampage in U.S. history took place on the Virginia Tech campus. Senior Seung-Hui Cho killed thirty-two people before committing suicide. Seventeen more people suffered gunshot wounds and other injuries.

Among those killed was someone Cass knew. "It's hard to explain just what this did to me, and I know I'm not alone," she writes on her blog. She says that at first she kept busy and did OK, but as the months went by

escue workers wheel a gurney into Virginia Tech's Norris Hall in the wake of the ᴘril 16, 2007, shooting rampage. Cass knew one of the victims personally and ᴇgan writing as a form of therapy in the aftermath of the attack.

she found she was emotionally unstable, crying if she tried to experience any emotion. Even visiting Disney World made her cry. She also started forgetting things so often that her husband had to keep repeating himself. "I stopped smiling," she writes. "I remember that now, just how little I smiled or laughed."

In the fall, she finally decided to see a therapist. The therapist gave her suggestions to find order and routine in her life, which she says worked a little. But the thing that really helped, she says, was something she had stumbled into accidentally—writing.

housands of people attend a candlelight vigil on the campus of Virginia Tech on
pril 17, 2007, the day after the shooting rampage.

THERAPY HAS BIG RESULTS

On the first anniversary of the shootings, Cass decided to write a story. She wanted to give her problems to a character and see how that character dealt with them because she felt she couldn't deal with her problems herself anymore. She set out to do that but never actually finished the story. However, a few weeks into that process, she woke up with an idea for a new story.

As she told *Ron Reads*, she was in a kind of haze from being asleep and was thinking about sirens (the mythological kind, not the kind on ambulances). She thought sirens would be really fun to write about, if only they had a reason to exist.

And then the idea came to her: what if the ocean was a living thing that eats people and needs beautiful women to

era Cass's first book, *The Siren*, was based on the ancient legend of
ystical women who lure sailors to their deaths, as illustrated in this 1875
ainting by Sir Edward Coley Burne-Jones.

get ships out so she can sink the ships and eat their crews? What if by doing so the ocean keeps the rest of the world alive? "That was the beginning of the whole thing, and those two paragraphs didn't even get used. But I was just so excited. I remember being at a party with all of my friends and I was just thinking that I want to go home," Cass recalled.

In *The Siren*, the sirens are girls who, as they are about to drown, are offered a bargain by the ocean: they will be allowed to live, in exchange for spending one hundred years luring ships to destruction. When their century-long sentences are over, the girls forget what they've done, but while doing it, they feel guilty. The justification for the ocean's actions is that it serves the world as a whole. Everyone needs water. The ocean has to exist.

Cass calls it "sad and mournful in a way, but also kind of beautiful. It's kind of creepy. But I really loved that story."

THE SIREN

It took Cass less than a month to write the first draft of *The Siren*, which in the end totaled more than one hundred thousand words. It took longer to revise and polish it, but soon she considered it finished and decided she was going to try to get it published.

She sent out more than eighty query letters — letters describing the book and providing her

DARKNESS IN
YA FICTION

On June 4, 2011, the *Wall Street Journal* published an article by Meghan Cox Gurdon headlined "Darkness Too Visible." The subhead noted that "contemporary fiction for teens is rife with explicit abuse, violence and depravity" and asked the question, "Why is this considered a good idea?"

In response, author Maureen Johnson started a Twitter hashtag, #yasaves, asking people to share how YA (young adult) books had saved them. Kiera Cass wrote a blog post detailing her reaction to the shooting at Virginia Tech, which was the direct impetus for her beginning to write. In it she notes that, "*The Siren* has language, a near rape, assault, and thoughts of suicide." And then she adds, "And it saved my life. It was my path back to normal... It's okay to talk about the bad stuff because the bad stuff is out there. It makes us weirdoes feel not quite so weird."

In another post, she notes that her husband, Callaway, has complained about some of the word choices in *The Siren*. She explained to him, she says, that that's just the way the characters talk—that it's not her fault: "I might be the one who dreamed up the world, but they are the ones who tell me how things go down. And while I might not be the kind of girl to drop an F-bomb into conversation on a day-to-day basis, one of my characters might be. If I try and censor them, the story just isn't as good."

writing credentials—to agents over a period of six months, asking if any of them would be interested in representing it to publishers. Only ten or so agents read it—and none of them, she told *I Am Meg*, was really excited about it. But Cass and her best friend had started doing what she calls "silly videos" on YouTube, and the followers of those videos knew that she had written a book and wanted her to make it available. Having failed to find an agent for it, she decided to publish it herself.

E-books weren't as popular then as they are now, so she set out to publish a physical book. She told *I Am Meg* it was a really good learning experience, and she learned a lot about trying to market herself, but she also said, "It's so difficult. I'm not good at making cover art! I'm not a great editor, I'm sure you will find grammar issues. As many times as I went through it, it's not the same as having...a copy editor."

SELF-PUBLISHING, PROS AND CONS

Not surprisingly, having self-published her first book before switching to traditional publishing, Cass has lots to say on the relative merits of each type of publishing.

Cass had, in her words from her blog, "a few doors slammed in the face of [her] first book," but, she adds, "there's a good reason for that."

As Cass puts it, the fact that anyone can publish a book has resulted in an onslaught of "absolute crap." That means that if you self-publish, even if your book is fantastic, it is part of a pile of "mediocre writing." No matter how hard you try, she says, you will never be able to polish your book to the same level that a professional editor can.

Cass says she still loves *The Siren*, and the fact that many of her fans still claim it's their favorite book, one they read again and again, makes her happy. But she knows that it's not as good as it could have been, and she doesn't feel it's as good as her current books, published by a traditional publisher.

But there are good things about self-publishing, she says. Top of the list? Speed. *The Selection*, her first traditionally published book, took years to see print, whereas *The Siren* took two months. The other big advantage is that there's no one to force the author to change anything he or she doesn't want to.

Yes, she says, sometimes self-published books are big breakout hits, but the chances of that happening are small. She says she treasures what she learned from the self-publishing experience—but she also says she could never go back.

As she told *Ron Reads*, self-publishing is great if you want your book out fast and you want complete control over it. "But for me, nothing beats having that support system of having your publisher and your agent and the people who are marketing it trying to find the best path for your book," she declared.

The Siren came out from iUniverse in July 2009. Cass was five months pregnant. After *The Siren's* publication, Cass worked very hard to market it, using, as she told *Writer's Digest*, what she had—a YouTube channel and a small but enthusiastic fan base—to make up for what she didn't have—shelf space in actual bookstores or major marketing help.

In the end, she said, although her fans made videos and she ran various Facebook contests, the thing that worked best turned out to be word of mouth. "I get a lot of 'so-and-so is a friend of so-and-so and they told me I had to read your book, and I love it and now my mom is reading it too!'" she told the magazine. What mattered least, she said, were the reviews on Amazon or Barnes & Noble. Although she asked readers to post reviews, and she's glad they did so, she doesn't feel it impacted sales.

On the other hand, she said, although it took a lot of hard work, the best thing she did was go through an index of young adult book blogs and set about getting reviews through them. Even though the only way she could offer *The Siren* was in PDF form, which limited the number of bloggers willing to read it, the ones who did had "great things to say," and she knows people who bought and read *The Siren* because of those bloggers.

Cass won't give out sales figures for *The Siren*. She says what felt like a huge accomplishment to her

iera Cass self-published her first book, *The Siren*, in 2009. She worked very hard market it herself since she didn't have the resources of a traditional publisher.

would probably look "kind of pathetic" in compari-son to the sales of any traditionally published novel. But she does note that on the day *The Siren* was released, she asked everyone she knew to go buy it on Amazon, which increased the sales rank to the point where she was contacted by two agents: "I think that's a must for anyone who chooses to self-publish…though it didn't work out it opened doors."

Cass said that even though sales of *The Siren* weren't perhaps "stellar," because the book is usually passed from hand to hand—after all, you can't just go into your local bookstore and buy a copy—its readers are people who have tended to stick around as Facebook friends, YouTube sub-scribers, and Twitter followers.

Writing *The Siren* had one other important effect on Cass: it got her in the habit of writing. And once she was in that habit lots of ideas started to come to her…including the one that would become *The Selection*.

FROM *THE SIREN* TO *THE SELECTION*

C ass told *Teen Vogue* that *The Selection* was inspired by two very different stories: the story of Esther, from the Bible, and the well-known fairy tale Cinderella.

In the Bible story, King Ahasuerus holds a 180-day feast during which he drinks too much and orders his queen, Vashti, to come to the feast and display her beauty to him and his guests. Queen Vashti refuses. The angry king asks his wise men what to do. One of them says that if the other women in the kingdom heard that Queen Vashti had refused to do what the king commanded her, they would become disobedient to their husbands, too, which would cause serious problems. The wise men urge the king to depose her.

Part of the inspiration for Kiera Cass's breakout book, *The Selection*, was the biblical story of Esther. In this painting by Caspar van den Hoecke, Esther is brought before King Ahaseurus, who chooses her out of all the women in his harem to be his new quee

The king takes their advice, but then he has to find a new queen. He decrees that beautiful young virgins from every province be sent to the palace. Each of the women undergoes a full year of beautification in his harem before being presented to the king. Each is given anything she wants to take with her from the harem when her turn comes. The king summons a woman in the evening and sends her back to the harem the next morning. If he is pleased with someone and wants to see her again, he calls her by name.

In the end, the king chooses Esther, who by virtue of her favor with the king is later able to protect her people, the Jews, from genocide instigated by an evil prince.

There are many versions of the Cinderella story, but the usual plot is that a young orphan, mistreated by her stepmother and stepsister, crashes a ball at the palace with the help of a magical godmother. The prince falls in love with her, but at midnight the beautiful magically produced clothes she is wearing turn to rags and she is forced to flee, leaving behind one of her glass slippers. The prince turns the kingdom upside down looking for her, forcing every young woman to try on the glass slipper. In the end he finds Cinderella, and the two are married and live happily ever after.

CLASSIC TALES AS INSPIRATION

Cass said she always wondered what was in Esther's heart: "Before she was taken away, did she maybe like the boy next door?" As she points out in her interview with *Ron Reads*, if Esther hadn't won, she would have been stuck in the harem for the rest

he Selection was also inspired by elements of the fairytale of Cinderella, best
own these days from the Disney movie version.

of her life. It could be, Cass said, that Esther had someone she'd always hoped to be with, but she had to let that love die. "I just thought that all of her sacrifices were kind of beautiful and interesting."

Cinderella, Cass points out, meets the prince and gets married, but she never actually asked for a prince. "She asked for a night off and a dress, that's all she wanted. So she gets this guy, we assume she's happy, but what if she's not? What if becoming a princess is way more than she intended to do and was way more stressful?"

Cass said those two stories kind of "married" in her head and gave her the idea to write about a girl who gets the attention of the prince but doesn't want it because she's already in love. As a result, she sees more of the world than she ever anticipated. That nugget of an idea became *The Selection*.

Cass said it took her a while to actually start writing the story because she didn't know where to place it. Originally, she thought of it like a fairy tale, set in the past, but she found that didn't really work. Instead, she ended up inventing her own country and placing the story in the future: she was driving one day when the word "Illéa" popped into her head, and suddenly she knew that was where the story took place. Once that happened, she started writing full-out.

THE SERIES BEGINS: *THE SELECTION* (NO SPOILERS)

The Selection is the story of America Singer, who has been chosen by lottery to enter a competition to become a princess and win the hand of the handsome Prince Maxon. For most of the thirty-five girls selected, this is the chance of a lifetime: an opportunity to escape their ordinary, regimented lives and enter a world of wealth and beauty.

For America, however, being selected feels more like a nightmare because it forces her to turn her back on Aspen, the boy with whom she is secretly in love, even though he is a caste below her. And the palace, despite being beautiful, is also under constant threat of savage rebel attacks.

But once America actually meets Prince Maxon, she begins to question herself and her dreams, as she gets a glimpse of a possible future she could never have imagined.

THE STORY BECOMES PART OF A TRILOGY

From the very beginning, Cass says she knew that the story would take more than one book to tell, although

she wasn't sure right away that it was going to be a trilogy. Once again, as with *The Siren*, her first draft took her about one month to write. However, the full process, from coming up with the idea to having a book she considered finished and ready to submit to publishers, took more like a year and a half.

One reason it took so long was that Cass ended up rewriting a lot of *The Selection*. Part of the problem, she told the *Literature Lion*, was that she was still in the same mindset as she had been with *The Siren*. In *The Siren*, her main character, Kahlen, was very bitter about

lthough the first draft of *The Selection* took Cass only about a month to write, the ook underwent so much rewriting that the full process from idea to finished novel ok more like a year and a half.

being forced to be a siren and wanted everyone to know that. "So when I started putting America's story on paper, I just thought that everything coming was from her. It took me a while to see how reserved she was, and that I was saying things that she didn't want said or pushing the story in a way it didn't really go," Cass said.

She provided more details to *Ron Reads*. She said when she finished the first book, she realized that although she thought she knew America, in fact she had gotten her completely wrong and had to go back and rewrite the book to make it consistent. One result was that by the end of the first book, the person America was supposed to end up with turned out not to be the same person Cass thought she would end up with in the beginning.

The Selection was very different from *The Siren* in other ways, Cass told *Writer's Digest*. For example, the first four chapters of *The Siren* involve Kahlen waiting for things to happen, and the readers wait with her. While Cass says she still wouldn't change that, she understands that it must have been a problem for agents, who typically ask to read the first three chapters. She also feels that the people in *The Selection* are a bit more real than the ones in *The Siren* and that the book overall is more commercial.

THE SEARCH FOR AN AGENT

Despite self-publishing *The Siren*, Cass wanted a traditional publisher for *The Selection*. So, as she had with *The Siren*, she began querying agents. She didn't query nearly as many, however, sending out letters to only thirteen. Two of those agents wanted to see it.

Of the two agents who expressed interest in *The Selection*, Cass chose Elana Roth, then at Caren Johnson Literary Agency (she's since started her own agency, Red Tree Literary). In her query, Cass had mentioned that she had published a book independently, provided some statistics about *The Siren*, and indicated that people had enjoyed the book. She also mentioned her YouTube channel. She hoped that telling agents about *The Siren* would prove to them that she had written a book before and could therefore write one again.

On March 22, 2010, just two months after she'd started sending out queries, Cass received the call from Roth offering to represent her. She writes on her blog that she had never actually prepared herself for the possibility of someone wanting to take on her novel. At the time, her son, Guyden, was three months old. She worried that he was going to be the "worst version of himself" during her call with Roth,

DYSTOPIAN?
WHAT'S THAT?

One of the major trends in young adult fiction in recent years has been stories set in dystopias. *Merriam-Webster* defines a dystopia as "an imaginary place where people are unhappy and usually afraid because they are not treated fairly," and that certainly applies to the world of *The Selection*.

But Cass admits that when she wrote the book, she didn't even know what a dystopian novel was. Roth made a reference to it in her phone call offering to represent the book, and after she got off the phone, Cass had to Google it to understand what it meant. "It was so embarrassing," she told *I Am Meg*.

Cass was aware of the most famous dystopian YA novel of them all, *The Hunger Games*, but she didn't read *The Hunger Games* until after *The Selection* came out. She still doesn't really consider *The Selection* a dystopian novel: she just thinks of it as a love story that happens to take place in the future, and she says the only reason it is set in the future is because she couldn't find any other setting for it. "In my head it's more like a fairy tale," she told *Teen Vogue*. "I've written a light, girlie book; *The Hunger Games* stories are far more epic and intense."

But having said that, she understands the attraction of dystopian novels. As she told *Safari Poet*, "I think dystopians are fun in the same way paranormal stories are fun. There's just enough reality to relate, but enough of a disconnect to be scared or excited or whatever that particular story is trying to bring out. It just gets you out of the real world for a while."

THE WORLD WILL BE WATCHING

THE
HUNGER GAMES

MARCH 23

Although her agent immediately thought of *The Selection* as a dystopian novel, Cass still thinks it's very different from the most successful dystopian novel of recent times, *The Hunger Games*, which is far more "epic and intense" than her "light, girlie book."

screaming in the background while she attempted to convince Roth that she could be both a new mother and a new author. "I don't know why, but that was one of my greatest worries, that motherhood would somehow knock me out of the race."

At that point Cass had a long list of questions for Roth and also wanted to talk to the other agent who had expressed interest. Also, there was no guarantee that Roth was even going to offer to represent Cass. Still, the author was impressed when Roth said that the book reminded her of "*Cinderella* meets *The Hunger Games* meets *The Bachelor*," because Cass had thought the very same thing the night before. "It wasn't some huge revelation, but I knew she got it."

They discussed how the author-agent relationship would work and how the complete trilogy would play out. Cass says that she wished with all of her heart that she had had all three books written so she could have just sent them all to Roth without having to flounder through a description of what she was "kind-of-almost-maybe-pretty sure" was going to happen.

And then, of course, after describing what she liked about the book, Roth told her everything she thought needed to be worked on. According to Cass, Roth kept worrying she was overwhelming the new author, but in fact for Cass that was the best part: "I knew it would have to be polished up, and I was grateful to have a set of professional eyes look at it and see ways to make it better."

Roth's offer to represent Cass came at the end of the phone call, but they both agreed Cass had to talk to the other interested agent first. If not for that, Cass wrote, she would have said yes right away.

Cass and Roth worked together on the novel to prepare it for submission to publishers. Just a few months after Roth agreed to represent Cass, HarperTeen editor Erika Sussman snapped up *The Selection*. Not only that, she signed Cass to a three-book deal, covering the entire trilogy.

CHAPTER FOUR

FROM UNKNOWN TO BEST SELLER

Cass soon discovered a big difference between self-publishing and traditional publishing. Whereas she had *The Siren* up for sale within a month of deciding to self-publish it, two years would pass between her signing the contract with HarperTeen and *The Selection*'s actual appearance on store shelves.

Still, she had plenty to keep her occupied in 2011: not just revisions on the first book, but writing the second book. And while all of that was going on, Cass was raising her young son. Of all of those tasks, she considered child-raising the most important. As she wrote on her blog, "I want to get Guyden through the year in one piece. Beyond that, anything is a bonus."

A CLOSE CALL

The new year began with a frightening near-tragedy. On January 20, 2011, Cass went with some friends to see the movie *The King's Speech*. As she was driving home, a deer jumped the guardrail. Cass swerved to avoid the deer, but the deer hit the front right of the car, pushing her deeper into the left lane. She wrote on her blog the next day, "The next part's a little unclear. I hit something, and I don't know if it was the man behind me hitting me, or me running into the other guard rail. All I know is that I whipped back and forth pretty quickly from three separate blows to the car and the only thing I could see was the exit sign. Blacksburg. Virginia Tech. Smart Road."

As she sat there gripping the wheel, she noticed a throbbing pain in her head: she had banged it against the window. A little dazed and confused, she pulled over to the shoulder and tried to collect herself. Then she heard a tap on the passenger-side window and saw her friend Jenna standing there. Jenna called 911, and Cass called her husband.

The car that had hit her from; behind was totaled, but its driver wasn't hurt. Remarkably, neither was the deer—at least, not seriously. After sitting by the side of the road for a while, it got up, jumped the guardrail, and ran back into the woods.

Fortunately, Cass was not seriously hurt either. She did have a bump on her head and a bruise on her shoulder, she found that her teeth and ribs hurt, and in general she felt achy. But, she assured her readers, "I'm totally fine and will be back to bugging you with silliness soon."

It was a close call. Had things gone differently that night, *The Selection* trilogy might never have seen the light of day.

"IN THE CLEARING"

During 2011, Cass also wrote a short story, "In the Clearing," for a YA dystopian anthology, edited by Paula Guran, entitled *Brave New Love: 15 Dystopian Tales of Desire*.

Cass found writing the story challenging. As she says on her blog, she started the story several times, only to cut off the first page or two because she realized it was unnecessary. What that meant, she says, was that she hadn't found the true beginning of her story.

As well, she says, since *The Siren* came in at one hundred thousand words and *The Selection* at eighty thousand, she found a word limit of thirteen thousand words restrictive. It took her multiple drafts to get it where she wanted to be, but, she writes, "The great thing about editing short stories is that you can read it in a few hours as opposed to a few days. And that's good because you can get rid of your bad ideas faster."

"In the Clearing" is told in alternating perspectives from a girl who lives in a very sheltered, quiet society and a boy who was chosen to live with a small group of outsiders in the woods. *Brave New Love* was released on February 13, 2012—just in time for Valentine's Day.

wo months before *The Selection* was published, Kiera Cass's short story "Into he Clearing" appeared in the YA dystopian anthology *Brave New Love: 15 ystopian Tales of Desire*, edited by Paula Guran.

Minooka Community High School
District 111
Channahon, IL 60410

THE ELITE PROVES CHALLENGING

In the spring of 2011, Cass and her husband went to New York, where they attended BookExpo America (BEA) so Cass could promote *The Selection*. She also had the opportunity to visit her publisher's offices, meet a lot of authors, and—best of all—meet her agent, Elana Roth, and her editor, Erika Sussman, in person.

In September, Cass turned in *The Elite*, the second book in the trilogy. As she told *USA Today*, the writing process for it was different from *The Selection*: "I wrote *The Selection* from start to finish, I wrote

2011, Cass traveled to New York for Book Expo America (BEA), the largest annual
ook trade fair in the United States, to promote *The Selection*. Many authors promote
eir books at BEA by speaking and signing copies.

my favorite parts of *The Elite* and then strung them together...*The Elite* has been kind of funny, though, because we ended up gutting it twice! The beginning and ending are basically the same but the middle has changed drastically from the original version."

On her own blog, Cass admits that the draft she submitted was nowhere near its final publishable state: "The first thing I handed over was so jacked up, Erika (my editor) didn't even bother doing line edits because I basically needed to gut the book and fix it...She put notes in the margin saying 'Why? Just why?' at one point. It was that bad."

THE SELECTION IS FINALLY PUBLISHED

In another blog entry prior to its publication, Cass talks about her doubts about *The Selection*, whose "pass pages" (pages sent to the author for proofing that are laid out like the final published book will be) she was going through in early October 2011. She wrote (in all capital letters), "THIS SUCKS! NO ONE IS GOING TO WANT TO READ THIS PILE OF JUNK! THIS IS JUST GOING TO WIND UP BEING VERY EXPENSIVE TOILET PAPER!"

She went on to say that she was nervous because the stories that she wrote to entertain

WORRYING ABOUT SUCCESS

All through 2011, Cass was in a strange kind of limbo: she'd sold her books, but nobody except her editor and agent had yet read them. On her blog, she mused about definitions of success for an author. She had read about seven-figure deals for two books that she didn't care for. It wasn't that she was unhappy with her own deal, but that she was wondering how she would ever know if she was any good at her job.

Would money constitute success? Or popularity? Hitting the *New York Times* best-seller list? Having a small but cult-like following? Movie rights sales? Multiple translations?

She wrote that she used to say the only thing she wanted was to catch someone she didn't know reading her book in public. But since there were no subways in Blacksburg to ride, and since she spent much of her time at home with her toddler, Guyden, she didn't actually see people very often in coffee shops and other places where they were likely to be reading.

"I say all this to say I don't know," she wrote. "Maybe *The Selection* will explode and people will start naming their kids Tuesday and Amberly, camp out for midnight movie releases, and make incredible T-shirts proclaiming their love for my characters. Maybe not." She went on to say that all she was trying to think about at that point was that "little spot on the YA shelf between Kristen Cashore and Kate Cassidy" that would be hers the next year.

After all, she wrote, "That's a lot to be excited about!"

herself were soon going to be in the hands of her readers, who could possibly hate them. Still, she said, she was very excited to share it, and even if in the end readers didn't respond to it, she wouldn't love it any less.

The Selection was released on April 24, 2012. By that time, Cass was pregnant again, with her daughter, Zuzu, who would be born in July. To celebrate the new book, she had a release party at the Christiansburg, Virginia, Barnes & Noble. Over the next month, she took part in a lot of events to promote *The Selection* at bookstores, libraries, high schools, and even her in-laws' house.

As Cass told *Ron Reads*, she thinks the positive reaction to *The Selection* took even her publisher by surprise. "I was waiting for the momentum to die, and I was ready to get people amped up and get excited again, and that moment never came. People read it and they got excited and they shared it with their friends. I was getting more Twitter followers and they were emailing me and it was this slow and constant growth." It began to show up on best-seller lists around the world.

In an interview with the *Daily Quirk*, she said that she found her fans the most exciting part about being a published author. "I would write and get the stories out just for me, even if no one liked

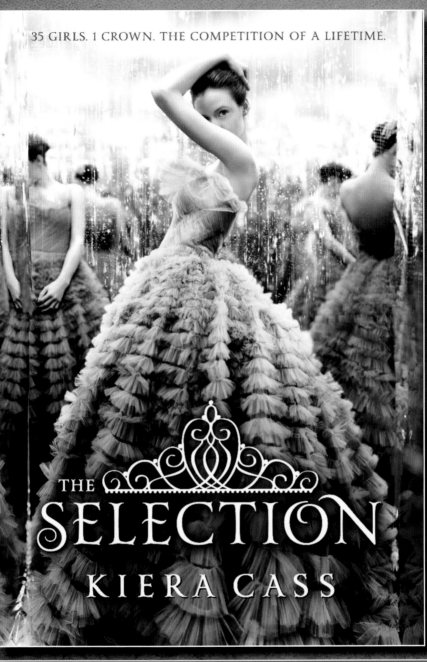

35 GIRLS. 1 CROWN. THE COMPETITION OF A LIFETIME.

THE
SELECTION
KIERA CASS

The Selection was finally released on April 24, 2012. Cass was very nervous about how it would be received, but before long it was showing up on best-seller lists around the world.

them. The fact that people make Twitter accounts for my characters and started writing fanfics has kind of blown my mind."

EVEN MORE SUCCESS WITH *THE ELITE*

Although her fans had a year-long wait between the release of *The Selection* and publication of *The Elite*, Cass gave them a stopgap story, in the form of an e-novella called *The Prince*, written from the perspective of Prince Maxon. She told the *Daily Quirk* that the novella came out of her editor asking her why Maxon was acting one way in a certain scene and why Aspen was doing something strange in another. She sat down and rewrote the scenes from the viewpoints of the boys, which helped her see how some things needed to be tweaked. "When the opportunity came to share Maxon's thoughts through a novella, it was exciting and scary. It's weird being in a boy's head, but (in some ways) he's less guarded than America."

Despite the positive reaction to *The Selection*, she continued to worry, as authors tend to do. She told *I Am Meg* that she lived with the fear that everyone was going to hate the second book. "People started making photo sets and role-playing sites and writing fan fiction, and I was like, 'Oh! You care! Oh gosh, what if

35 GIRLS CAME TO THE PALACE. ONLY 6 REMAIN.

THE ELITE

A SELECTION NOVEL

KIERA CASS

#1 *New York Times* BESTSELLING AUTHOR

he second book in the trilogy, *The Elite*, came out one year after *The election*, on April 23, 2013, and debuted at number one on the *New York mes* best-seller list.

you hate [*The Elite*]? I don't want
you to hate this!'"

Her fears were groundless.
The Elite came out one year
after *The Selection*, on April 23,
2013, and debuted at number
one on the *New York Times*
best-seller list. She found out
in a very public way. As she
told *Ron Reads*, she was at the
Romantic Times book conven-
tion. She had just picked up a
package of Starbursts on her
way into a panel she wanted to
sit in on and was chewing the
candy when her publicist told
her the good news. "There's a
bunch of people in the room and
she pulls it up on her iPad and I
sort of start crying and jumping
around," Cass said. Her reaction was captured on video. She
said she missed the panel she'd
wanted to listen to because she
went out to the hallway to cry,
and then she called her husband
and her mother. "I was totally shocked because there
were a lot of great authors on that list."

Cass promoted her books at local Barnes & Noble bookstores. These stores often feature author readings and Q & A sessions, such as this one with coauthors Bobby Williams and Mariel Heminngway, to promote forthcoming books.

But she went on to say that although being a *New York Times* best-selling author was awesome and amazing, it still didn't change what she had to do every day. "I still have to change diapers, I still have to get dinner to the table. Someone has to do the laundry. Who? *The New York Times* bestseller."

TAKING THE BOOKS OVERSEAS

One exciting development for Cass in 2013 was the opportunity to tour internationally. Before she was published, she said that the thing she was most looking forward to was the opportunity to tour. On August 3, she appeared at National Bookstore in Glorietta 1, a shopping mall in Manila,

ass has a huge following in the Philippines among teen girls. In 2013, more
an six hundred fans turned out at the National Bookstore in Glorietta 1 for
ass's appearance on her first-ever trip overseas.

the Philippines, where she was met by more than six hundred screaming fans. According to *I Am Meg*, they held her books, dressed as her characters, and showed her fan art of their favorite moments. It was not only Cass's first overseas book signing but also her first overseas trip ever.

About two months before the trip to the Philippines, the Casses moved from Blacksburg to Christiansburg, Virginia. The move finally provided Cass with more office space. As she told *Ron Reads*, she had gotten in the habit of working in the local Panera bakery-café because their house had gotten "kind of cluttered when we started having children."

A few months before *The One* came out on May 6, 2014, fans of *The Selection* trilogy could pick up another treat: *The Selection Stories: The Prince & The Guard*. Published in February 2014, this volume contains the novella *The Prince* and a second novella, *The Guard*, told from Aspen's point of view.

ONTO THE NEXT

Even before it was published, presales had already pushed *The One* near the top of the Amazon best-seller rankings in teen fiction. According to *Publishers Weekly*, "Fans of Cass's Selection trilogy won't be disappointed with this satisfying final installment." But Cass is not resting on her laurels. *The Queen*, another novella in *The Selection* world, is a prequel about Prince Maxon's mother, Queen Amberly. Meanwhile, Cass's next project will be a duology about unwanted children who are sent to an academy to be raised as companions, who are then purchased by people to befriend their children.

She provided some details to *Entertainment Weekly*: "If you have an insecure child, you can buy them a fat best friend. Or if you have a son who is an incredible athlete, you can buy him someone to train with who would never be allowed to compete against them because they're like a second class. There's a lot of restrictions in their lives, because their life is devoted to another person—they can't have family of their own, relationships of their own, careers of their own. So it's about this girl and her living for other people."

"It's a little bit darker than *The Selection*," she told *I Am Meg*, "but still a love story."

It's already been an amazing journey—and yet it's one she's really just begun—for someone who never set out to be a writer. "Once I started writing, I felt like an idiot," she writes on her website. "How had I not known I loved this all along? Seriously. Dancing, singing, acting, history…it's all just story telling. And I love it."

CRITICAL RESPONSE: THE GOOD, THE BAD, AND THE UGLY

O ne thing Cass admits she was not really ready for was the critical reaction to her work—especially negative criticism. She thought she was prepared for it, but she really wasn't. As she told *Ron Reads*, because she and her friend used to make videos on YouTube, they were used to people being critical for no reason: "People are really mean on the Internet...And it doesn't matter."

But it was different with her first book. She was happy when some people were really excited about the book on the basis of the ARCs (advance reading copies) that were sent out, but then, she said, "when some people came in really harsh, it was a bit devastating because I was not prepared. I just didn't know what to do with it."

A PUBLIC RELATIONS MISSTEP

Unfortunately for Cass, this unpreparedness played out in public on the social media/book review site Goodreads. What happened was recounted in a story by Karen Springen in *Publishers Weekly*. Dated January 19, 2012, still months before *The Selection* was actually published, it's headlined "Should Authors and Agents Weigh In on Citizen Reviews?"

On January 13, Springen wrote, a one-star review of *The Selection* appeared on Goodreads. Reviewer Wendy Darling wrote, "[I] didn't find a single aspect of this story that I enjoyed" and noted, "the story ends on a cliffhanger, as if there were so much going on in this one book, it could not be contained in a single volume."

Cass and her agent, Elana Roth, exchanged messages on Twitter about how to deal with the negative review, apparently under the impression that they were exchanging private messages instead of posting them publicly. In one message, Roth called Darling a vulgar name. She went on to say that she had gone through all the Goodreads reviews and "liked" all of the four- and five-star ones

ONLY 1 GIRL CAN WIN THE CROWN.

THE ONE

A SELECTION NOVEL

KIERA CASS

#1 *New York Times* BESTSELLING AUTHOR

The One, the final novel in Kiera Cass's best-selling trilogy, was published in Ma 2014. Cass is already at work on her next project.

in an effort to move those reviews closer to the top of the list of reviews (reviews with the most likes are placed at the top of the list by default).

This ignited a firestorm of criticism from members of the Goodreads "citizen reviewers" community. Darling told *Publishers Weekly*, "Some of these authors don't seem to have PR training or common sense."

Both Roth and Cass apologized to Darling. In a post on July 6, 2012, on her blog, Cass said the entire incident was unfortunate. She wrote, "When that happened, I was a newbie hoping for piles of awesome and learning to deal with the fact that some people were just going to hate my book. It was hard to see a negative review at the top of my Goodreads page at the time, but it's probably not something I would notice these days."

To *Ron Reads*, she said, "Haters, over all, are a good thing. If everybody loves your book, then you are not reaching enough people. People disliking it is proof that you've reached a large audience. It's difficult to deal with sometimes but it's good news when people don't like your book."

THE CRITICS WEIGH IN

Professional reviewers were generally much more positive. In its review, *Publishers Weekly* called *The Selection*, "A cross between *The Hunger Games* (minus the bloodsport) and *The Bachelor* (minus the blood-sport)." The review noted that the book employs "multiple conventions of the dystopian romance genre," but added, "That said, it's a lot of fun" and called its heroine, America, easy to root for.

Publishers Weekly liked the second book, too, calling the series "deliciously entertaining" and offering only the minor criticism that "America's 'whatever shall I do?' musings can get a little taxing." All in all, the reviewer wrote, "Cass delivers another round of enjoyable, clean, romantic fun."

chool Library Journal said *The Elite* reads like a mix between *The Bachelor*, *The unger Games*, and *Downton Abbey* (*seen here*).

Another major reviewer of young adult novels, *School Library Journal*, called *The Selection* "an engrossing tale of high-stakes competition and the emotional turmoil of being true to oneself." It added, "Fairy-tale lovers will lose themselves in America's alternate reality and wish that the next glamorous sequel were waiting for them."

Of that sequel, the magazine wrote, "*The Elite* seems like a mix between *The Bachelor*, *The Hunger Games*, and *Downton Abbey*...Some parts of the story lack background information, but possibly the next book will answer these questions. There is a lot going on here, but readers can pick up this book and, for the most part, make sense of it."

WRITING HONESTLY

Among the plethora of reviews, Cass herself has noted, are some that call her anti-feminist and complain that America doesn't seem like a strong female character. But Cass pushes back hard against that claim. As she told *Ron Reads*, "I think it's really ridiculous that for a woman to be considered strong, she has to take on all the characteristics of a man. That is stupid." She notes that America's greatest strengths to her are that she makes sacrifices and that she protects the people that she can. That effort alone, Cass says, is really

IT'S GOING TO BE A TV SERIES!... OR NOT

In February 2012, Cass announced very exciting news: *The Selection* had been picked up by the CW television network for a potential series. She had originally heard the news back in July 2011. As she wrote on her blog, she was "driving to Toddler Talk with Guyden, minding my own business, tra la la la la," when her agent called to tell her that Warner Bros., one of the owners of the CW, was interested in optioning *The Selection*. (When a production company options a property, it pays the author for the rights for, typically, about a year, during which the company explores the possibility of producing it as a TV series, TV movie, or motion picture. Many projects that are optioned are never actually produced.)

After she talked to her agent, Cass spoke with people at Warner Bros. and, by the end of the conversation, felt "pretty encouraged." She was pleased with the idea of a television series as opposed to a movie because whereas in movies you have to cut things out of books, in television series you can actually explore more elements of the created world. Warner Bros. even agreed to hire her as a creative consultant. She later indicated she was very happy with the script written by Elizabeth Craft and Sarah Fain for the pilot, which, by the time Cass posted about the

(*continued on the next page*)

(continued from the previous page)

potential series on her blog in February, was already in the works and scheduled to be shot in Vancouver, Canada. Even so, Cass sounded a note of caution, pointing out that the show still might not happen.

That proved to be prescient. Although in the end two pilots were shot, the first in Vancouver and the second (with some casting and script changes) in Budapest, Hungary, the CW passed on the series. At present, there are no plans for either a movie or television adaptation of *The Selection* trilogy.

strong. "I don't try to write strong female characters. I just try to write honest female characters."

In the end, Cass says, she isn't writing for critics or readers, but for herself. "I just stumbled into writing out of necessity. I think this was just given to me in a time of need and it changed me. I'm so grateful for it and what I'm able to do and I'm grateful that anybody cares or agrees or appreciates.

"It's really beautiful and wonderful."

ON KIERA CASS

Birth Date: May 19, 1981

Birthplace: South Carolina

Current Hometown: Christiansburg, Virginia

Education: BA in History, Radford University

First Publication: *The Siren*, 2009

Marital Status: Married Callaway Cass, 2004

Children: One son, Guydan, and one daughter, Zuzu

Hobby: Making YouTube videos

Website: http://www.kieracass.com

Blog: http://www.kieracass.com/journal

Twitter: @KieraCass

Facebook: https://www.facebook.com/pages/
Kiera-Cass/356163161993

Tumblr: http://www.partylikeawordstar.tumblr.com

YouTube: http://www.youtube.com/user/KieraCass

Pinterest: http://www.pinterest.com/kieracass

Vine: https://vine.co/u/957312019692961792

Instagram: http://www.instagram.com/
partylikeawordstar

Quote from Kiera Cass: "In 2007, my world was
shaken by a local tragedy, and I took it pretty
hard. Over the course of the following year, I tried
a lot of things to get myself together resulting in

me sitting down to write a story where my character had to deal with my problems so I wouldn't have to. The distance from my head to the page helped me step back a bit and cope with all the things I was feeling. I ended up not finishing that story because I woke up from a nap with the idea that would become *The Siren* and HAD to get that written. After I got into the habit of writing, lots of ideas came, including *The Selection* and handful of others that are waiting their turn. Once I started writing, I felt like an idiot. How had I not known I loved this all along? Seriously. Dancing, singing, acting, history...it's all just story telling. And I love it."

ON KIERA CASS'S WORK

The Siren. Bloomington, IN: iUniverse, 2009.
Released: July 9, 2009
Summary: Kahlen is a siren, saved from drowning by the ocean in exchange for a hundred years of service luring ships to destruction to feed the ocean's hunger and keep the world alive. But when Akinli, a human, enters her world, she can't bring herself to live by the rules anymore.

The Selection. New York, NY: HarperTeen, 2012.
Released: April 24, 2012
Summary: For thirty-five girls, the Selection is the chance of a lifetime: an opportunity to escape their rigid society, live in an opulent palace, and compete for the heart of Prince Maxon. But for America Singer, it's a nightmare, forcing her to turn her back on her secret love, Aspen. Then she meets the Prince and begins to realize the life she's dreamed of may not compare to a future she never imagined.

The Elite. New York, NY: HarperTeen, 2013.
Released: April 23, 2013

Summary: The original group of thirty-five girls has been narrowed down to the six Elite. The closer America gets to the crown, the more she struggles to figure out where her heart truly lies. She's desperate for more time, but while she's torn between Aspen and Maxon, the rest of the Elite know exactly what they want—and America's chance to choose is about to slip away.

The Selection Stories: The Prince & The Guard. New York, NY: HarperTeen, 2014.
Released: February 4, 2014

Summary: Before America arrived at the palace to compete in the Selection, there was another girl in Prince Maxon's life. *The Prince* opens the week before the Selection begins and follows Maxon through the first day of the competition. In *The Guard*, readers get an inside look at Aspen's life as a guard within the palace walls—and the truth about a guard's world that America will never know.

The One. New York, NY: HarperTeen, 2014.
Released: May 6, 2014

Summary: America has made her choice. Now she's prepared to fight for the future she wants.

The Selection

"A cross between *The Hunger Games* (minus
the bloodsport) and *The Bachelor* (minus the
bloodsport)...A lot of fun."—*Publishers Weekly*

"Cass's immensely readable debut novel is a less
drastic *Hunger Games*, with elaborate fashion
and trappings. The fast-paced action will have
readers gasping for the upcoming sequel."
—*Booklist*

"An engrossing tale of high-stakes competition
and the emotional turmoil of being true to oneself...Fairy-tale lovers will lose themselves in
America's alternate reality and wish that the
next glamorous sequel were waiting for them."
—Jamie-Lee Schombs, *School Library Journal*

The Elite

"Deliciously entertaining...all in all, Cass delivers
another round of enjoyable, clean, romantic
fun for readers who would love to spend just
one day in America's pampered shoes."—
Publishers Weekly

"America is becoming more mature and teenagers will easily relate to her growing pains. While
the plot is somewhat repetitive, readers will

enjoy the same caliber of writing found in *The Selection*. The love triangle is subtle and the characters are likable and relatable." —Natalie Gurr, *Children's Literature*

"A welcome addition to the series...America's character is more fully developed; in simple prose readers see the complicated feelings that can evolve when one feels love for two individuals—albeit a very different kind of love for each." —Erin Forson, *VOYA*

The One

"The final book in Cass's 'Selection' series begins in the midst of a rebel attack on the palace. The heroine, America, is one of four remaining ladies competing in the selection process in this dystopian saga. Through bravery and a strong character, America has won the people's hearts...Fans of this series will not be disappointed by the ending. Major plotlines are tied up, and questions left unanswered in the previous installment are resolved here. The star-crossed duo's relationship has its many ups and downs, but their love for each other remains." —Jesten Ray, *School Library Journal*

"Fans of Cass's Selection trilogy won't be disappointed with this satisfying final installment...

America has the right mix of sass and heart, and her over-the-top royal treatment is enough to make any reader who has ever played dress-up envious. Cass wisely keeps the Selection
decision uncertain until the very end, keeping readers on the edge of their seats to find out who Maxon will finally choose as his bride."
—*Publisher's Weekly*

"*The One* finds gutsy protagonist America Singer as one of four remaining Elite vying to be chosen by Prince Maxon as the Princess of Illea. Packed with romance, action, intrigue, and bravery sure to infuriate King Clarkson but endear her to the populous, Mer's journey keeps readers enthralled ...This expertly woven, suspense-filled tale is sure to please lovers of reality television, dystopian societies, romance, and royalty, and it already has a firm fan base eagerly awaiting its release."—*VOYA*

1981 Kiera Cass is born in South Carolina.

1999 Cass graduates high school, then takes the fall semester off to perform in local shows and teach at a theater camp.

2000 She enrolls in Coastal Carolina University in January, majoring in musical theater. That fall, she follows a boy to Radford, Virginia, enrolling in Radford University and switching her major to music.

2001 She switches her major to communications, becomes an RA, and meets her future husband, Callaway Cass.

2002 She switches her major to history.

2004 Kiera marries Callaway Cass.

She graduates from Radford University with a degree in history.

The Casses move to Blacksburg, Virginia.

2007 On April 16, Seung-Hui Cho, a senior at Virginia Tech, shoots and kills thirty-two people and wounds seventeen others in two separate attacks, then commits suicide. Among those killed is someone Cass knows personally.

2008 On April 16, Cass begins writing a story. A few weeks into it, she wakes up with an idea for a new story, which will become her first book, *The Siren*.

She sends ends eighty query letters to agents with no success and decides to self-publish.

2009 *The Siren* is released from iUniverse in July Cass gives birth to her first child, son Guyden. She begins writing *The Selection*.

2010 Agent Elana Roth calls Cass and offers to represent her.

Editor Erika Sussman at HarperTeen signs Cass to a three-book deal.

2011 On January 20, Cass hits a deer while driving home from a movie and is rear-ended by another car.

She writes a short story, "In the Clearing," for a YA dystopian anthology, edited by Paula Guran, entitled *Brave New Love: 15 Dystopian Tales of Desire*.

Warner Bros. options *The Selection* for a possible TV series.

2012 Cass and her agent are caught up in controversy when comments they made about a one-star reviewer on Goodreads become public and the subject of a *Publishers Weekly* story.

On April 24, *The Selection* is published.

On July 9, daughter Zuzu is born.

2013 On April 23, *The Elite* is published and debuts at number one on the *New York Times* best-seller list.

The Casses move to Christiansburg, Virginia.

Cass makes her first overseas trip, to the Philippines, where she is greeted by hundreds of excited fans.

2014 *The Selection Stories: The Prince & The Guard* is published, comprising two novellas and additional bonus material.

The One, the concluding book in *The Selection* trilogy, is published.

The Queen, another novella in *The Selection* world, is published.

AGENT An individual who submits an author's books to a publisher on the author's behalf and helps negotiate the contract, for a share of the payment.

ANTHOLOGY A collection of short stories, poems, or essays by different authors, usually tied together by one theme.

ARC Advance reading copy. A bound copy of a book's uncorrected page proofs, sent out to reviewers well in advance of the book's publication so reviews can appear before or at the same time as the book is published.

CASTE Social class.

CONCURRENTLY Happening at the same time.

COPY EDITOR An editor who closely reads a manuscript, correcting errors in spelling, grammar, and style.

DEPRAVITY Evil or immoral behavior.

DIVA In opera, the main female singer. The word has also become attached to any famous and successful woman who is very attractive and fashionable, especially a performer or celebrity.

DRAFT A completed version of a manuscript, usually subject to further editing.

DRY-HEAVING Retching.

DUOLOGY A two-book series of novels, telling a complete story.

DYSTOPIA An imaginary place where people are unhappy and usually afraid because they are not treated fairly.

E-BOOK A book published as a file that can only be read on an electronic device.

EXPLICIT Content that is intended for mature audiences, often depicting nudity, profanity, or sexual situations.

FAN ART Art created by fans of a work representing characters or scenes from the work.

FAN FICTION Fiction created by readers featuring characters from a published novel, TV series, or movie.

FANTASTICAL Odd or strange.

GENOCIDE Deliberate killing of a group of people based on their religion or ethnicity.

GOODREADS A social media site where readers share their reviews and ratings of the books they read.

HAREM A group of women, often living together, associated with one man.

IMPETUS Motivation.

INSTIGATE To bring about.

LIMBO A period of waiting for a result.

LINE EDITS The process of reading a manuscript closely and tightening the writing for improvement.

MAJOR The subject of concentration for a university student, in which he or she will receive a degree upon graduation.

MINOR The subject a university student studies in addition to his or her major. It may or may not be related to his or her major.

NOVELLA A complete story longer than a short story but much shorter than most novels.

OPTION The exclusive right, usually purchased for a fee, to turn a book into a movie, TV movie, or TV series. Options are time-limited and must be renewed at regular intervals if not acted upon.

PERSPECTIVE The point of view of a character.

PILOT A television program produced as a prototype of a series being considered for adoption by a network.

PLAYLIST A series of songs selected from multiple sources.

PRESALES Books ordered before their release date.

PRESCIENT Being able to see or envision events before they happen.

QUERY LETTER A letter sent to an agent or publisher asking if he or she is interested in representing or publishing the book described therein.

RESIDENT ASSISTANT (RA) A trained leader who supervises those living in a dorm or other community situation.

RIFE Widespread.

SELF-PUBLISHING Publication of a book by the person who wrote it.

TRADITIONAL PUBLISHING Publication of a book by a company specializing in publishing, marketing, and distributing books.

TRILOGY A complete story told over the course of three books.

TURBULENT Confused or disordered.

VIGIL A watch conducted by a group to pray or pay respect.

YOUNG ADULT A marketing term for books aimed at younger readers, typically teenagers.

American Library Association (ALA)
50 East Huron Street
Chicago, IL 60611
(800) 545-2433
Website: http://www.ala.org
The American Library Association (ALA) is the oldest and largest library association in the world, providing information, news, events, and advocacy resources for members, librarians, and library users. The ALA offers information and guidance to readers and researchers regarding any number of acclaimed authors.

Canadian Children's Book Centre (CCBC)
40 Orchard View Boulevard, Suite 217
Toronto, ON M4R 1B9
Canada
(416) 975-0010
Website: http://www.bookcentre.ca
The CCBC provides resources and publications for children's authors, teachers, and parents interested in encouraging young readers.

Canadian Library Association (CLA)
1150 Morrison Drive, Suite 400
Ottawa, ON K2H 8S9
Canada

(613) 232-9625
Website: http://www.cla.ca
The Canadian Library Association advocates for
the nation's library network and provides support to Canadian authors.

HarperTeen
HarperCollins Publishers
195 Broadway
New York, NY 10007
(212) 207-7000
E-mail: harperteen@harpercollins.com
Website: http://www.harperteen.com
HarperTeen publishes Kiera Cass's novels and offers
information about HarperTeen authors and their
books, including samples, cover art, and more.

Kiera Cass
Website: http://www.kieracass.com
The author's official website features news,
events, information about the books, answers
to frequently asked questions, and Cass's regularly updated journal.

National Council of Teachers of English Promising
Young Writers Program (NCTE)
1111 W. Kenyon Road

Urbana, IL 61801-1096
(877) 369-6283
Website: http://www.ncte.org/awards/student/pyw
The Promising Young Writers program represents
NCTE's commitment to early and continu-
ing work in the development of writing. The
school-based writing program was established
in 1985 to stimulate and recognize students'
writing talents and to emphasize the impor-
tance of writing skills among eighth-grade
students. Students who are eighth-graders
in the present academic school year are eli-
gible to be nominated for the Promising Young
Writers program. Students must be nominated
by their teachers.

National Writing Project (NWP)
University of California
2105 Bancroft Way #1042
Berkeley, CA 94720-1042
(510) 642-0963
Website: http://www.nwp.org
The National Writing Project focuses the knowl-
edge, expertise, and leadership of our nation's
educators on sustained efforts to improve
writing and learning for all learners. Writing
in its many forms is the signature means of

communication in the 21st century. The NWP
envisions a future where every person is
an accomplished writer, engaged learner,
and active participant in a digital, intercon-
nected world.

Red Tree Literary
Elana Roth
320 7th Avenue, #183
Brooklyn, NY 11215
Website: http://www.redtreeliterary.com
Kiera Cass's agent's website offers additional
   information about Cass's books and news of
   Roth's other clients.

School Library Journal
160 Varick Street, 11th Floor
New York, NY 10013
(646) 380-0700
Website: http://www.slj.com
School Library Journal aspires to be an accel-
   erator for innovation in schools and public
   libraries that serve the information, literacy,
   and technology needs of twenty-first century
   children and young adults. *SLJ* produces
   resources, services, and reviews that make
   library and education professionals savvier and
   communities stronger.

Young Adult Library Services Association (YALSA)
50 East Huron Street
Chicago, IL 60611-2795
(800) 545-2433
Website: http://www.ala.org
The Young Adult Library Services Association
   is a national association of librarians, library
   workers, and advocates whose mission is to
   expand and strengthen library services for
   teens. YALSA awards the Michael L. Printz
   Award, an annual prize for a book that
   exemplifies literary excellence in young
   adult literature.

WEBSITES

Because of the changing nature of Internet links,
Rosen Publishing has developed an online list of
websites related to the subject of this book. This
site is updated regularly. Please use this link to
access the list:

http://www.rosenlinks.com/AAA/Cass

FOR FURTHER READING

Cass, Kiera. *The Elite*. New York, NY: HarperTeen, 2013.

Cass, Kiera. *The One*. New York, NY: HarperTeen, 2014.

Cass, Kiera. *The Selection*. New York, NY: HarperTeen, 2012.

Cass, Kiera. *The Siren*. Bloomington, IN: iUniverse, 2009.

Cass, Kiera. *The Selection Stories: The Prince & The Guard*. New York, NY: HarperTeen, 2014.

Collins, Suzanne. *Catching Fire*. New York: Scholastic, 2009.

Collins, Suzanne. *The Hunger Games*. New York: Scholastic, 2008.

Collins, Suzanne. *Mockingjay*. New York: Scholastic, 2010.

Condie, Ally. *Crossed*. New York: Dutton, 2011.

Condie, Ally. *Matched*. New York: Dutton, 2010.

Condie, Ally. *Reached*. New York: Dutton, 2012.

Dashner, James. *The Maze Runner*. New York: Delacorte Press, 2010.

Guran, Paula, ed. *Brave New Love: 15 Dystopian Tales of Desire*. Philadelphia, PA: Running Press, 2012.

Meyer, Marissa. *Cinder*. New York: Macmillan, 2012.

Meyer, Marissa. *Cress*. New York: Macmillan, 2014.

Meyer, Marissa. *Scarlet*. New York: Macmillan, 2013.

Oliver, Lauren. *Delirium*. New York: HarperCollins, 2011.

Roth, Veronica. *Allegiant*. New York: HarperCollins, 2013.

Roth, Veronica. *Divergent*. New York: HarperCollins, 2011.

Roth, Veronica. *Insurgent*. New York: HarperCollins, 2012.

Westerfeld, Scott. *Extras*. New York: Simon & Schuster, 2011.

Westerfeld, Scott. *Pretties*. New York: Simon & Schuster, 2011.

Westerfeld, Scott. *Specials*. New York: Simon & Schuster, 2011.

Westerfeld, Scott. *Uglies*. New York: Simon & Schuster, 2011.

Ang, Raymond. "A Causal Encounter with Kiera Cass." *Philippine Star*, August 30, 2013. Retrieved January 17, 2014 (http://www.philstar.com/young-star/2013/08/30/1148571/casual-encounter-kiera-cass).

Brissey, Breia. "Kiera Cass Talks Her YA Debut 'The Selection'." *Entertainment Weekly*, April 27, 2012. Retrieved January 17, 2014 (http://shelf-life.ew.com/2012/04/27/the-selection-kiera-cass/2).

Brissey, Breia. "'The Elite': Kiera Cass Talks About the Sequel to 'The Selection.'" *Entertainment Weekly*, April 23, 2013. Retrieved January 17, 2014 (http://shelf-life.ew.com/2013/04/23/kiera-cass-the-elite-the-selection-sequel).

Cass, Kiera. "FAQ." Retrieved January 17, 2014 (http://www.kieracass.com/faq).

Cass, Kiera. "Journal." Retrieved January 17, 2014 (http://www.kieracass.com/journal).

Cass, Kiera. "So What Happened Was..." Retrieved January 17, 2014 (http://www.kieracass.com/about-me).

The IamMEG Team. "A Candid Interview with Kiera Cass in Manila." *I Am Meg*, August 22, 2013. Retrieved January 17, 2014 (http://iammeg.ph/a-candid-interview-with-kiera-cass-in-manila).

BIBLIOGRAPHY

Literature Lion. "Review & Interview: The Selection by Kiera Cass." July 5, 2012. Retrieved January 17, 2014 (http://theliteraturelion .blogspot.ca/2012/07/review-interview -selection-by-kiera.html).

Matricinno, D. "From Self-Published Author to 3-Book Deal: The Story of Kiera Cass." *Writer's Digest*, August 11, 2010. Retrieved January 17, 2014 (http://www.writersdigest.com/ editor-blogs/there-are-no-rules/digitization -new-technology/from-self-published-author -to-3-book-deal-the-story-of-kiera-cass).

Parkin, Lisa. "The Selection Author Kiera Cass on Princess Kate, Self-Publishing and *The Elite.*" *Huffington Post*, May 20, 2013. Retrieved January 17, 2014 (http://www.huffingtonpost .com/lisa-parkin/the-selection-author-kier_b _3288199.html).

Potts, Jessie. "Interviews: Kiera Cass and Cornelia Funke." *USA Today*, April 24, 2013. Retrieved January 17, 2014 (http://www.usatoday .com/story/happyeverafter/2013/04/24/ cornelia-funke-kiera-cass-interviews/2107363).

RonReads. "Author Interview: Kiera Cass." September 23, 2013. Retrieved January 17, 2014 (http://ronreads.com/author-interview/ author-interview-kiera-cass).

Safari Poet. "Author Interview: Kiera Cass." February 2012. Retrieved January 17, 2014 (http://safaripoet.blogspot.ca/2012/02/author -interview-kiera-cass.html).

Springen, Karen. "Should Authors and Agents Weigh In on Citizen Reviews?" *Publishers Weekly*, January 19, 2012. Retrieved January 17, 2014 (http://www.publishersweekly.com/paper-copy/ by-topic/childrens/childrens-industry-news/ article/50268-should-authors-and-agents-weigh -in-on-citizen-reviews.html).

Tishgart, Sierra. "Young Adult Author Kiera Cass on *The Selection*." *Teen Vogue*, April 2012. Retrieved January 17, 2014 (http://www .teenvogue.com/entertainment/books/2012 -04/kiera-cass-the-selection).

Walker, Mallory. "An Interview with Author Kiera Cass." *Daily Quirk*, April 17, 2013. Retrieved January 17, 2014 (http://thedailyquirk.com/2013/04/17/ an-interview-with-author-kiera-cass).

INDEX

ABOUT THE AUTHOR

Edward Willett is the award-winning author of numerous books of fiction and nonfiction for children, adults, and young adults. He's previously written biographies of authors J.R.R. Tolkien and Orson Scott Card, as well as musicians Jimi Hendrix, Johnny Cash, and Janis Joplin. His fiction includes *Marseguro*, winner of the 2009 Aurora Award for best Canadian science fiction novel, the new YA fantasy series *The Shards of Excalibur*, and the fantasy series *The Masks of Aygriman* (written as E.C. Blake). Willett is also a professional actor and singer. He lives in Regina, Saskatchewan, Canada, with his wife and daughter. You can find out more about him at www.edwardwillett.com, @ewillett on Twitter, or on Facebook.

PHOTO CREDITS

Minooka Community High School
District 111
Channahon, IL 60410

DATE DUE

			PRINTED IN U.S.A.